For the *Love* of the Mets

An A–to–Z Primer for Mets Fans of All Ages

Foreword by Rusty Staub

Written by Frederick C. Klein

Illustrated and designed by Mark Anderson

Coming to New York was the best thing that happened in my career. I'm proud to have a share in the Mets' storied legacy. In the beginning, there was Casey. Stengel was more than just a manager. He was a pioneer, a trailblazer, a spokesman, and a public-relations tool for the team. He did all that with humor, and made the Mets "Amazin'."

There is "Tom Terrific." He is "the Franchise." He is the Babe Ruth, Walter Johnson, Stan Musial, Ted Williams, and Sandy Koufax of the Mets. He is Tom Seaver, the greatest player in the almost half-century of their existence.

"Kid" was the whole package as a catcher. Strawberry hit tremendous, majestic, tape-measure home runs to distances that few hitters could reach. Kooz was the real deal as a pitcher. Keith Hernandez had that stifling defense that brought a new dimension to the art of playing first base. Mike Piazza will be elected to the Hall of Fame and he will be regarded as the best offensive catcher in the history of the game. And none was as big a part of the Mets' legacy as kooky, wacky, flaky, lovable Tug McGraw.

The future of the Mets belongs with David Wright, a special player who has a chance to rank right up there with any third baseman who every played; Jose Reyes, who comes with just about every talent you want; and heavy-hitting Carlos Beltran, the best center-fielder in Mets history, who can carry the Mets to the Promised Land.

—Rusty Staub

Outfielder Rusty Staub spent two stints with the Mets (1972–75 and 1981–85) during a 23-year major-league career in which he batted .279, hit 292 home runs, and was a six-time All-Star. The redheaded New Orleans native, dubbed "Le Grande Orange," was a fan favorite at Shea Stadium, especially after he helped lead New York to the 1973 World Series against the A's, then batted .423 in a losing cause despite playing with a separated shoulder. Since retiring, Staub has maintained a high profile in New York through his successful restaurants and his charitable foundation, which raises money for the families of police officers and firefighters killed in the line of duty.

"A" is for the "Amazin's,"

Who made many gaffes,
But also were good for
A whole lot of laughs.

The New York Mets began life in 1962 as an expansion team ungenerously stocked with has-beens and never-weres. They finished last in the National League in five of their first six seasons and lost more than 100 games in each. But managed by the wry **Casey Stengel** (who first referred to the "Amazin' Mets") and fielding lineups of plucky strivers, they nonetheless came off as lovable to a growing legion of fans. The classic early Mets story involved "Marvelous" Marv Throneberry, a bumbling first baseman, who was called out for missing second base after hitting a triple. When Stengel charged out of the dugout to protest the call he was restrained by his third base coach, Cookie Lavagetto. "Don't bother," Lavagetto said. "He didn't touch first, either."

"B" is for Beltran,

Who patrols the big green.
At the plate he is strong;
In the field he is keen.

Carlos Beltran made a grand show in the 2004 playoffs as a Houston Astro, hitting eight home runs and batting in 14 runs in that team's 12-game pennant try. The next winter he attracted considerable interest as a free agent before signing a seven-year, $119 million contract with the Mets. Injuries hampered his 2005 campaign, but the native of Puerto Rico rebounded strongly the next three seasons, **hitting a total of 101 home runs, driving in 340 runs,** and establishing himself as a top-flight center fielder.

"C" is for Carter,

The last piece in the scheme
That brought home the title
And fulfilled the dream.

Gary Carter, nicknamed "the Kid" for his always-youthful enthusiasm for baseball, was an All-Star catcher for the Montreal Expos when he was traded to the Mets after the 1984 season. In New York, he continued apace, completing the lineup that would win the 1986 World Series. That year he hit 24 home runs and drove in 105 runs during regular-season play, hit two homers in Game 3 of the World Series against Boston, and started the game-winning rally in Game 6 with a single. He would play five seasons for the Mets before concluding a Hall of Fame career back in Montreal.

"D" is for

Darryl,

Who could hit the long ball,
But his skills couldn't save him
From a very hard fall.

Lanky Darryl Strawberry came out of inner-city Los Angeles as the No. 1 choice in the 1980 amateur draft. He hit the major leagues running with the Mets in 1983 and starred for the next eight years, blasting a team-record 252 home runs with his signature high knee cock and looping, powerful swing. Off-field problems began to plague him, and though he continued to play, his last nine seasons in the Bigs never equaled his early year bests. His post-baseball life has been marred by illness, drug and driving arrests, and a prison term.

"E" is for Elster,

A boon to the club.
He went 88 games
With nary a flub.

Kevin Elster was the prototypical slick-fielding shortstop while holding down the starting spot at the testing position for the Mets during most of his 1986–1992 stay with the team. In one stretch during the 1988 and 1989 seasons he completed 88 straight games without an error, setting a major-league record that the great Cal Ripken broke in 1990.

"F" is for Fernandez,

The Portly "El Sid." Fans still remark
About the things that he did.

At times weighing close to 250 pounds, **Sid Fernandez** filled out his baseball uniform. He also posted impressive pitching numbers during 15 major-league seasons, 10 of which (1984–1993) were with the Mets. The left-handed sidearmer had wicked stuff, recording 114 career wins and 1,743 strikeouts. Most impressively, his 6.85 hits-allowed-per-nine-innings average ranks among the best ever. The Hawaiian's best year was with the Mets' 1986 champs, when he had a 16–6 won-lost mark and 200 strikeouts. He gave up just one run in 6⅔ innings in the '86 World Series, fanning 10.

"G" is for Gooden,

The swift "Dr. K."
He'd set up a batter
Then blow him away.

Few pitchers have burst onto the big-league scene as splashily as Dwight Gooden.
Flashing a high-90s fastball and sharp-breaking curve, the lean right hander won 17 of 26 decisions with 276 strikeouts in 1984 as a 19-year-old rookie. The next year he had a 24–4 won-lost record and a league-leading 268 strikeouts. But while he pitched effectively for a half-dozen seasons thereafter and won 19 games in 1990, he never fully matched his earlier performances. Injuries contributed to his decline, and like teammate Strawberry he fell into a drug habit that followed him into retirement.

"H" is for

Hernandez–

For batters, a pit.
Everything hit Keith's way
Wound up in his mitt.

Top first basemen generally distinguish themselves as hitters, and while **Keith Hernandez had a .296 batting average over 17 major-league seasons**, seven of them with the Mets (1983–1989), he made his mark mainly with his glove. His range was so wide that he could play farther off the bag than others and still cover the foul line. His arm was so strong that his teams routed outfield relay throws through him. And he was so good at turning sacrifice bunts into force-outs or double plays that many foes simply abandoned the tactic against him. Some experts consider him the best ever to play the position.

"I" is for Innings,

The standard is nine.
But if the game's tied
Then more are just fine.

"J" is for Johan,

For whom teams bid high.
'Cause his luggage contained
More than one "Cy."

For most of his seven seasons with the Minnesota Twins, Johan Santana **was considered the best pitcher in the American League**—and he had two unanimous Cy Young Awards (in 2004 and 2006) to prove it. When the Twins put him on the trading block after the 2007 campaign they received many bids. Signed by the Mets to a seven-year, $137.5 million contract in the winter of 2007, the Venezuelan lefty swiftly verified his worth by posting a 16–7 won-lost record in 2008 and leading the majors with a 2.53 earned run average.

"K" is for Koosman,

Who with chips on the line
Came through like a champ
In 1969.

Jerry Koosman **won 19 games as a rookie in 1968** and 17 the next year in teaming with Tom Seaver to pitch the "Miracle Mets" to a World Series title for a franchise that had never finished higher than ninth in the National League. The lefty was at his best in the 1969 Series, throwing 8⅔ innings in the Mets' 2–1 Game 2 win over the Baltimore Orioles and going all the way for a 5–3 victory in the fifth and deciding contest. Over a 19-year big-league career—12 years of it in New York—he won 222 games and had an earned run average of 3.36.

"L" is for

Leiter

A pitcher with guile
With the 2000 Mets,
He made the fans smile.

Al Leiter, from Toms River, New Jersey, is another left-handed pitcher who figured prominently in a Mets pennant run. **In 2000, his 16 regular-season victories were a team high,** and he pitched effectively throughout the playoffs, helping the Mets reach the World Series. In seven seasons with the Mets (1998–2004) the control specialist had a 95–67 won-lost record and never posted a losing year.

"M" is for McGraw,

Always there to relieve.
All New York loved his slogan:
"You Gotta Believe!"

Frank "Tug" McGraw **was a left-handed relief specialist for the 1969 and 1973 Mets pennant winners.** His best pitch was a screwball, a backwards curve few pitchers can master. McGraw also was known for enjoying himself off the field and issuing colorful locker-room quotes. Of his salary he once said, "Ninety percent I'll spend on good times, women, and Irish whiskey. The rest I'll probably waste." He coined the Mets' 1973 battle cry, "You Gotta Believe!" His son, Tim, is a successful country music artist.

"N" is for Nelson,

A broadcasting pro.
His voice on the airwaves
Helped make the team grow.

Early New York Mets teams may have been amateurish but when the club wanted someone to lead its broadcasting team it turned to a man who'd already established a national media reputation. Wearing his trademark loud sports jackets, Tennessee-born Lindsey Nelson was the Mets' primary radio and TV voice from 1962 through 1978. When he departed, his sidekicks Bob Murphy and Ralph Kiner carried on in his stead. Nelson and Murphy are in the Baseball Hall of Fame as broadcasters, and one-time slugger Kiner is there as a player.

"O" is for Olerud,

A sweet-swinging lefty.
His power was good.
His average was hefty.

John Olerud, who stood 6'5", had a left-handed swing that made batting coaches sigh with pleasure and pitchers groan in pain. His power to all fields and sharp batting eye gave him a distinguished, 17-season major-league career. In his three seasons with the Mets (1997–1999) he set single-season team records for batting average and on-base percentage (.354 and .447, respectively, in 1998) and walks (125 in 1999). Two Golden Glove Awards attested to his fielding ability at first base.

"P" is for

Piazza—

Played catcher, batted right.
Groove a fastball to him and
It was gone—out of sight!

One of baseball's best-hitting catchers, Mike Piazza's 396 career home runs at the position is a record. Eight of his 16 seasons (1998–2005) were with the Mets, where he established a team career mark for slugging percentage (.542) and is second in home runs (220) and runs batted in (655). He's considered a sure Hall of Fame selection when he becomes eligible in 2012.

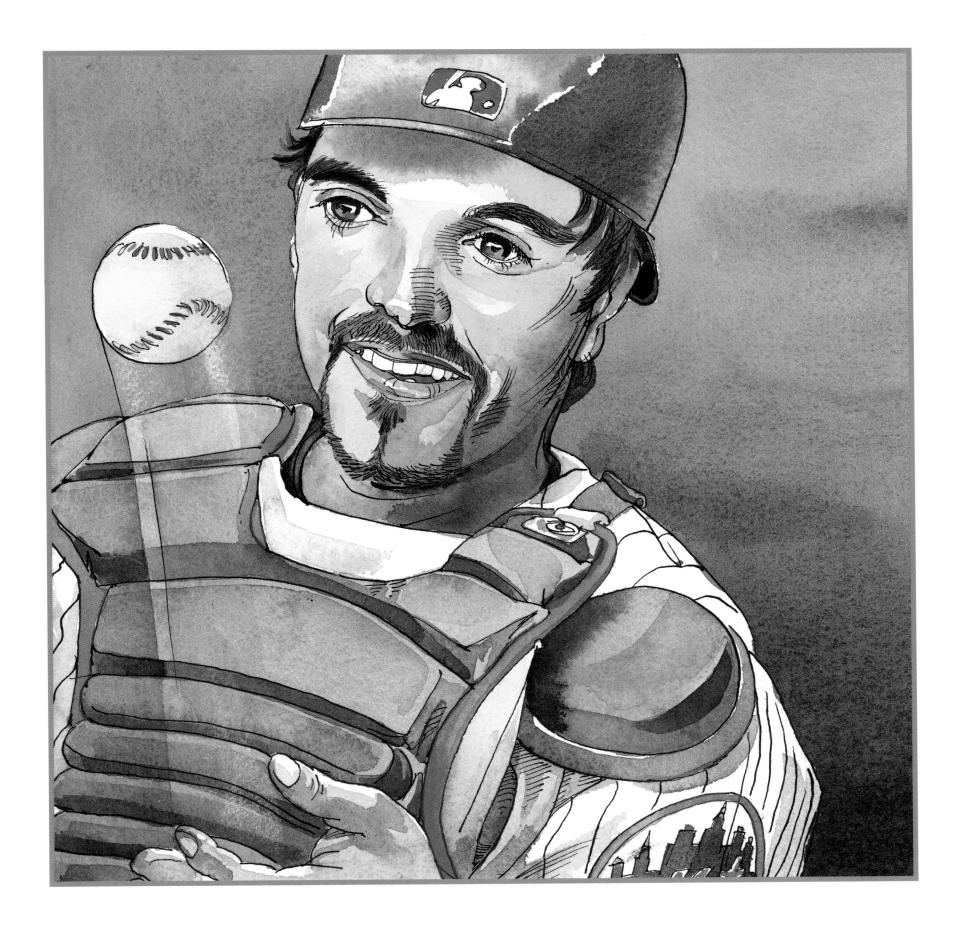

"Q" is for

Quest,

For the NL crown.
Get anything less and
The town feels let down.

"R" is for Reyes,

On the bases, a whiz.
He gives the Mets' lineup
A big shot of fizz.

Jose Reyes is one of the fastest players to wear a Mets—or any other club's—uniform. Just 21 years old when he became the team's starting shortstop in 2005, he stole 258 bases and accumulated 779 hits in his first four full major-league seasons, while also making the National League All-Star team twice.

"S" is for Shea,

Whose brief made the case: When the NL expanded, New York got a place.

When the Giants and Dodgers left New York after the 1957 season, Mayor Robert Wagner formed a committee to get the National League back in town. Lawyer **William A. Shea** quickly took charge of the group. He first tried to persuade another city's team to come, but that failed. He proposed that the league expand from its longtime limit of eight teams, but that failed, too. Then he hatched the idea of forming a new baseball entity, the Continental League, with a New York team as its anchor. That got the owners' attention. They reversed themselves on expansion, with New York and Houston getting teams in 1962. He became part of the new club's ownership. The Mets' first permanent home, Shea Stadium in Queens, was named in his honor.

"T" is for Tom

That's "Mr. Terrific."
For victories and Ks
He was truly prolific.

The Mets' change from awful to awesome began in earnest in the winter of 1966 when they signed Tom Seaver, a smart, sturdy right-handed pitcher from the University of Southern California. After just one year in the minors Seaver came to New York and immediately became the anchor of the Mets' starting staff, winning 16 games each in 1967 and 1968. The next year he posted a 25–7 won-lost mark in leading the team's championship charge. He would spend 11 of his 20 major-league seasons with the Mets and record most of his 311 career wins and 3,640 strikeouts with the team.

"U" is for

Umpires,

Who, though fans may howl,
  Still have the last word:
Safe or out, fair or fowl.

"V" is for Valentine–

This skipper was smart.
The teams that he managed
Showed plenty of heart.

Bobby Valentine **was an infielder with the Mets in 1978 and returned to manage the team from 1996 through 2002**. His 1999 club won 97 regular-season games and beat Arizona in the divisional playoff series. Then it lost to Atlanta in the league-championship series, four games to two, after dropping the first three games and battling back from a 0–5 deficit before losing Game 6 in 11 innings. His 2000 Mets won the franchise's first National League pennant in 16 years before losing to the Yankees in the "subway" World Series. Tough and competitive, Valentine also had a mischievous side. Once, after being ejected from a game, he snuck back into the dugout wearing civilian clothes, dark glasses, and a grease-pencil mustache.

"W" is for

Wright–

At third base, a fixture.
In the batting-crown races
He's right in the picture.

David Wright **has been everything a team could want in a third baseman—and more.** Since coming up in 2004 at age 21, he's hit for both average and power and has been rock-steady defensively. He was an All-Star in 2006, 2007, and 2008 while capturing Gold Glove and Silver Slugger awards. In 2008 he batted .302 while setting personal season highs in home runs (33) and runs batted in (124).

"X"

marks the spot
In the dirt behind first,
Where Billy Buck's boot
Sparked the Mets' winning burst.

The most-dramatic play in Mets' history came at Shea Stadium in the sixth game of the 1986 World Series against the Boston Red Sox. Behind three games to two and facing elimination, the Mets trailed 5–3 going into the bottom of the tenth inning. After their first two hitters were retired the Mets scored a run on three singles and tied things on a wild pitch. Mookie Wilson's grounder to first base seemed sure to end the inning and continue the contest, but it went through Bill Buckner's legs and enabled Ray Knight to score the winning run. Two nights later, the Mets won Game Seven 8–5, and the Series.

"Y" is for Yogi,

No jester was he,
When the Mets barely missed
In '73.

Yogi Berra is best known as a Hall of Fame catcher with the 1950s Yankees and for spouting head-scratching malapropisms such as "Ninety per cent of the game is half mental," but he also was a solid baseball man with good managerial instincts. His 1964 Yankees won the American League pennant and **he managed the 1973 Mets to the National League crown and into the seventh game of the World Series against the Oakland A's.** The '73 Mets' postseason run was in some ways more remarkable than their winning 1969 effort. The team finished the regular season with a mediocre 82–79 record, 17 games worse than the Western Division–leading Cincinnati Reds, but it upset the powerful Reds in the NL title series and led the A's three games to two before succumbing.

"Z" is the sound
Someone makes when he snoozes.
A Mets fan stays loyal
Even when his team loses.

When have the Mets been in the World Series?

1969

Defeated the Baltimore Orioles, four games to one

1973

Lost to the Oakland A's, four games to three

1986

Defeated the Boston Red Sox, four games to three

2000

Lost to the New York Yankees, four games to one

*Purchase high quality 18x24 archival prints and
T-shirts of your favorite Met at:*

This book is available in quantity at special discounts for your group or organization. For further information, contact:

Triumph Books
542 South Dearborn Street
Suite 750
Chicago, Illinois 60605
312. 939. 3330
Fax 312. 663. 3557

Printed in China
ISBN 978–1–60078–204–6